A STORYTELLER'S GUIDE TO A JOYFUL HOLIDAY SEASON

Thanksgiving |Advent |Christmas |New Year

Tony Agnesi

Virtu Press

Wadsworth, Ohio

2012–2024 Tony Agnesi

Printed in the United States of America

ISBN- (Virtu Press)

ISBN: 979-8-218-31819-2

The author is donating 100 percent of the net proceeds from this book to the charities and ministries he and his wife support. Many of these charities and ministries are mentioned in his books.

Dedication

To the Agnesi and Amicone Families: Holidays are a special time and they evolve over our lifetime. I remember fondly celebrating Christmas with my parents, aunts, uncles and cousins. Later, I remember celebrating with my family and my wife, Diane's families, splitting our time Christmas Day with an early meal with one family and a late meal with the other.

For many years Diane and I hosted Christmas and had a party with our entire family a day or two later. It was a fun family reunion and our kids and grandkids got to see their family.

Now, we are the older generation and the holiday celebrations have been passed on to our adult children and grandchildren. We take new joy in spending the holidays with Matthew and Teresa, Mark and Jackie and our two grandsons, Nico and Luca, and granddaughter Gianna Marie.

CONTENTS

Chapter 3- Christmas

Chapter 4- New Year

Introduction

Over the past 13 year, I have been writing and blogging and podcasting. My blog, *Finding God's Grace in Everyday Life,* was my first attempt at writing since college. As a storyteller, I have been asked by family and friends to share my stories in writing. The blog was, to my surprise, a success. It was names multiple times as one of the top 100 Catholic blogs and was the runner-up in the 2015 Bloggy Awards in the category of spirituality. With that encouragement, I have since written five books, *A Storyteller's Guide to a Joyful Holiday Season* is my sixth and fourth in the Storyteller's Series.

Over the year the majority of comments, emails and letter I have received have mentions the holiday stories that I shared on my blog and in my books. Many have asked if I would put together a book of holiday only stories, reflections, prayers and quotes from over the years.

This book is the results of the curation of over a decade of writing. I hope you will enjoy the reflections and that they may add joy to your holiday season!

CHAPTER ONE

Thanksgiving

In All Things Give Thanks

I read an article recently that said the words *thanks, thanksgiving or give thanks* are used in the bible 162 times. The word *thanks* alone, 73 times and *thanksgiving* 25 times. I guess that means the bible views **giving thanks** as an important element of Christianity.

But we seem to live in a society of want! Gratitude has left secular society to the extent that we are raising a self-absorbed, entitlement generation.

It's not until something bad happens; an illness, disease, the death of a loved one, a disaster, flood, tsunami, or wild fire that it shocks us into understanding just how good we have it. The richest 300 people in the world have more wealth than the 3 billion poorest. Even the poorest of

Americans has more than 80% of the world. We all have reason to give thanks.

In the past few weeks, several of my friends have had bad health news; a brain tumor, renal failure, a cancer reoccurrence, and a sudden death of a loved one. In each instance, the persons affected spoke words of gratitude. They were thankful that their problem wasn't as bad as the person in the next hospital bed. They were grateful that the issue was discovered early and the some of the best doctors in the country were available to help. They were grateful, for family and friends who rallied around them in their time of need. And, they were grateful, to a loving and forgiving God for a chance to beat the odds.

Why don't more people get it? Why does something have to happen to get our attention? Is gratitude simply a cute photo slide that we "like" on a Facebook post and never give another thought? Is it just sappy sentimentality?

Or is it a way of life? Should we, as the Bible says, *"give thanks in everything!"*

"In all circumstances give thanks, for this is the will of God for you in Christ Jesus." -- 1Thessalonians 5:18

St. Rose of Lima in her beautiful writings speaks of the grace that come to those who are afflicted with suffering. Suffering is the true stairway to paradise, through the cross and resurrection of our Lord, Jesus Christ. As a cancer survivor, I can attest to that! I am a better person today for having experienced it.

As St. Rose wrote; *"Our Lord and Savior lifted up his voice and said with incomparable majesty: 'Let all men know that grace comes after tribulation. Let them know that without the burden of afflictions it is impossible to reach the height of grace. Let them know that the gifts of grace increase as the struggles increase. Let men take care not to stray and be deceived. This is the only true stairway to paradise, and without the cross they can find no road to climb to heaven.' "* *–from the writings of St. Rose of Lima*

As you read this, offer up some thanks to God for all that you have. Not for what you need, but those things you already have been blessed with.

Lord, thank you for this day, and thank you for everything that you have blessed me with. Make me a good steward of these many blessings and to share my good fortunes with those in need.

Reflection: *Has there been a trying time in your life that God's grace helped you get through? Do you agree with St. Rose that grace flows to the afflicted and hurting?*

The Empty Chair

"He will wipe every tear from their eyes, and there shall be no more death or mourning, wailing or pain, [for] the old order has passed away." –Revelations 21:4

"The LORD is close to the brokenhearted, saves those whose spirit is crushed." —Psalm 34:19

Thanksgiving and Christmas are the happiest times of the year. We get together with family and friends, exchange gifts, share wonderful meals, and enjoy the holidays.

But, for many of us, the loss of a loved one makes this a sad and even depressing time. Let's face it; every one of us will have a holiday where there is an empty chair.

The loss of a spouse, parent, grandparent or a child can be devastating enough, but the holidays have a way of magnifying the sadness. Add the cold and snow and the fact that it gets dark earlier, and just getting out of the house seems like an insurmountable task.

So, what can we do? How can we not only get through the holidays, but find joy in the season?

Here are some ideas that might help:

1. **Let the traditions evolve.** If you have always hosted Christmas at your house, let someone else host. Especially for those who have lost a spouse, this is the perfect time to pass on the hosting responsibilities to an adult daughter or son. After all, they have families and starting a new Christmas tradition will take the pressure off of you

and let you think less of what was and more of right now and what can be.

2. **During the Holiday season manage your loneliness.** Stay active and get out of the house. Accept invitations from friends, even if you don't feel quite up to it. Try volunteering at a homeless shelter, or help serve Thanksgiving dinner to the less fortunate in your town.

3. **Accept your feelings, it's ok to grieve.** A wonderful way to remember a lost loved one is to light a candle, hang their favorite Christmas ornament of the tree, or make a charitable donation in their name. And feel free to talk about your loved one with family at the holidays. They too want to keep the deceased spirit alive and part of family traditions. It gives them permission to share some wonderful stories or photos that will warm your heart.

4. **Take care of your health.** During these difficult times it is easy to slack off in your self-care. Get up, shower, get dressed, work out, take a walk, and attend Mass or anything else to get moving. Remember to eat regular meals. Often, the loneliness of the holidays causes us to miss meals, eat all

of the wrong things or to drink too much
coffee or alcohol.

5. **Stay close to Our Lord.** As psalm 34
reminds us, the Lord is close to the brokenhearted.
He is there for us   at Mass, in the reception of
the sacraments, in the rosary and reading
scriptures. He will get us through these difficult
times if we just reach out in prayer.

And, that is the message of Christmas. We are not
alone, not when the night is darkest, the wind
coldest, or the world seemingly most indifferent.

With God's help, we can make it through the
holidays together, and celebrate our lost loved one
whose memory remains, in spite of the empty
chair.

God bless you my friend.

Reflections: *What do you think of Tony's ideas for
remembering a loved one? Do you have a tradition at the
holidays to remember those that have past? What can we do
to help a person who has experienced a loss this year?*

Our Thanksgiving Pizza

*A man gave a great dinner to which he invited many.
When the time for the dinner came, he dispatched his servant
to say to those invited, "Come, everything is now ready."*

But one by one, they all began to excuse themselves. Luke 14:16-18

In June, my wife Diane and I celebrated our 51st wedding anniversary. In those 51 years, we have had some interesting holiday gatherings but none like the one in Atlanta, Georgia that never happened.

We were a young married couple and seeking a new adventure in Atlanta. I had just received a job offer to program one of the first talk radio stations in the country, Ring Radio.

I can still remember our drive to Atlanta. We followed each other down I-85, she in her Monte Carlo and me in my Honda Civic. We were young and very inexperienced. Diane had barely been out of the state of Ohio and our honeymoon was the first time either of us had been out of the country.

In Atlanta, we made friends quickly. Many folks were just like us, northerners who had come to the south for work. All had left families in places like Ohio, Michigan, Pennsylvania and Wisconsin and had to make friends in our new environment or be alone. So, people were very friendly.

Diane and I joined the local Catholic Church, a small gathering of mostly northerners that met for Mass in a small activity center with an Irish priest, a missionary to the US! It was 1975 and Vietnam was still fresh in the countries consciousness. I was in the Army Reserves and had drill weekends in

18

Rome, Georgia as well as summer camps in
Wisconsin, Virginia and other posts. One of our
church's outreaches was to adopt a few South
Vietnamese families, who had settled in our area.

Life in Atlanta was going pretty well until we
realized that we would not be going home for
Thanksgiving. My new job meant that we would
be celebrating the holiday away from our family in
Ohio. Then, Diane had a great idea!

"I am sure that there are others couple like us who
won't be making it home to their families this
Thanksgiving, let's host a big Thanksgiving dinner
here."

"That's a great idea," I exclaimed! I could already
taste Diane's great cooking.

We invited four other couple to join us and
everyone accepted. Diane prepared the menu, we
bought a turkey and I received a holiday ham from
my employer, so there would be plenty of food for
everyone.

The day before our big feast, one of the couples
called to tell us they wouldn't be making it to the
dinner. Her husband was able to get last minute
plane tickets and they were going home to
Michigan. Well, there were still three couples
joining us.

That night, while Diane was making preparations
and doing some baking, the phone rang and you

guessed it, another couple called to cancel. "Boy, there sure is going to be a lot of food for six people," I said with a little disappointment in my voice.

Thanksgiving morning, the phone rang twice more, each with the same news that our guests would be spending Thanksgiving somewhere else. We were in shock! The expectations of the good food shared with friends vanished as I hung up the phone for the final time.

The next hour or so was spent with shared tears and disappointment. Now what? What do we do with a turkey, a ham, and all the side dishes and desserts?

Then, Diane had another idea.

"Let's box it all up and deliver it to the Vietnamese families our church had sponsored. They can celebrate our U.S. holiday with their families," she said choking back tears. "At least someone will be having a family holiday." We did just that.

It is difficult to describe the amazed look on the faces of the Vietnamese families as we dropped off our American feast. Although they were still learning English, their tearful thank you, head bows, and smiles were all we needed to know that we were not only doing the right thing, but that somehow God was directing the entire story.

When we returned to our apartment, we realized that it was late and we still had not eaten. "What do you want on the pizza?" I asked, as I dialed the local pizza shop. "Pepperoni and green peppers" was her reply. Thirty minutes later we were enjoying our Thanksgiving meal, alone, but laughing, glad to be together, and somehow knowing that God had used us to deliver a miracle to families who will forever remember their first Thanksgiving Day.

Reflections: *Have you ever felt that God was directing your actions? Do you remember a time when things didn't go as planned? How did you react?*

A Thanksgiving Prayer

This is one of my favorite Thanksgiving Day Payers. We have used this at our Thanksgiving meals for many years. In these turbulent economic times, this prayer seems so appropriate for those of us who have so much. God bless you and Happy Thanksgiving!

Oh, God, when I have food,
help me to remember the hungry.
When I have work,
help me to remember the jobless,
When I have a warm home,
help me to remember the homeless.
When I am without pain, help me to remember

those who suffer.
And remembering, help me to destroy my
complacency and bestir my compassion. Make
me concerned enough to help, by word and
deed, those who cry out for what we take for
granted.

Samuel F. Pugh

A Thanksgiving Rosary

Fifteen years ago, on the day I first was diagnosed
with colon cancer, I returned home from the
doctor's office to an e-mail from Paul McManus
with the 7 Great Prayers. This e-mail later became
a book by the same name that I hand out to friends
and acquaintances.   One of the prayers is a simple
"Thank you, God….."

I remember praying that short prayer that night,
"Thank you God for the early diagnosis, thank you
for a loving wife who will help me get through,
thank you for my faith, thank you for my friends"
and so on until my little prayer of gratitude ended
90 minutes later. I couldn't believe how blessed I
am and how many things Our Lord has given me!

I've shared that story over the years a friend, Pat,
said that he remembered my story and used this
simple prayer during adoration. He thanked God
for something on each bead as he prayed the

rosary. As Pat prayed the rosary, he always had a thank you ready before the next Hail Mary began. When he had completed the rosary, he still could think of many more. He said this was one of the most meaningful rosaries that he had prayed in a long time.

Since then, I have prayed many Thanksgiving Rosaries and have shared the idea with people everywhere. The questions I am always asked is "Do you ever run out of thank-yous?" The answer is never!

What a great idea for Thanksgiving! Pray a rosary with a grateful "Thank You" on each bead. I'm going to try it this week on Thanksgiving Day, and I invite you to do the same.

Reflection: What do you think? Are you willing to give it a try?

Thank God for Dirty Dishes

My grandma, Frances, was a wise woman. As an immigrant to this country, she worked hard to raise her family and she did very well. Grandma had an old Italian saying, a poem, or a song, for any occasion that helped her to make a point with her kids and grandchildren. Over the years these sayings reminded us of Grandma Agnesi. We love sharing them with family members. This week, with Thanksgiving fast approaching, my cousin Linda reminded me of a poem that Grandma would recite to the females in the family when it was time to do the Thanksgiving dishes. (Usually, the guys were sleeping in front of the 19-inch black and white television in the parlor watching the football game.)

I think I learned some of my storytelling abilities from Grandma! Here is the poem she shared, written by Mary Arlis Stuber:

Thank God for dirty dishes;
They have a tale to tell.
While others may go hungry,
We're eating very well
With home, health, and happiness,
I shouldn't want to fuss;
By the stack of evidence,
***God's* been very good to us.**

CHAPTER TWO

....

ADVENT

Welcome to Secular Advent

And do this because you know the time; it is the hour now for you to awake from sleep. For our salvation is nearer now than when we first believed; the night is advanced, the day is at hand. Let us then throw off the works of darkness [and] put on the armor of light. Romans 13:11-12

Welcome my friends to Secular Advent! For those of you who are not familiar with the holiday season, it began several years ago and has grown into the biggest secular holiday of the year.

Secular Advent used to begin on Black Friday. Now it begins with Grey Thursday, right after Thanksgiving dinner, because greed can't wait for an entire day of giving thanks, especially when we forget who to thank!

The worst moment for the atheist is when he is really thankful, and has nobody to thank.—Dante Gabriel Rossetti

There are other minor holidays during Secular Advent, as well, like Small Business Saturday, and Cyber Monday, but Secular Advent continues all the way until Return Unwanted Gifts Week!

For those of you, like me, who celebrate the Christian Advent, you need to understand that Secular Advent is the antithesis of The Christian Advent.

Secular Advent asks us to speed up and spend money now! Christian Advent asks us to slow down and prepare for the coming of our savior Jesus Christ.

Secular Advent asks us to spend money we don't have on things we don't need, under the pretense that "it was on sale!" Christian Advent asks us to be thankful for what we have and to give to those who have little.

Secular Advent asks us to fight for our rights for the last big screen television at Walmart, even if it means we have to kill for it, or at least start a riot. Christian Advent asks us to pray for peace in the world.

Secular Advent reminds us that seven year-old's need an iPhone 11 and both the Xbox and Play Station gaming systems because they deserve it.

Christian Advent reminds us that some children will have no gifts at Christmas and wouldn't it be nice to buy something for a child who has little or nothing.

As for me, I prefer the Advent of our Christian faith. And, so as not to get caught up in the hype of this secular holiday, here are a few things I am going to do. Maybe you might try these too:

1. I'm going to **slow down and enjoy the advent season**, enjoy the beauty of winter closing in, snowfall, and family and friends.

2. As a Catholic, I'm going to **attend mass every day** this advent season and focus on the coming of Jesus, not only on Christmas day, but his second coming as well.

3. I'm going **to increase my prayer time**, especially to pray for those who will be sad at this special time of year because they have lost a loved one this year.

4. I'm going to **help someone in need**, a family member, a friend or just a name from the giving tree or Salvation Army list.

My protest will be a quiet one, a silent one. I will just choose not to participate in the madness. Instead, I'll try to concentrate my thoughts and deeds on *throwing off the works of darkness and putting on the armor of light.*

Please join me this Advent.

....

Advent or Advil

> Come to me, all you
> who labor and are
> burdened, and I will
> give you rest.
> (Matthew 11:28,
> NAB)

All the way to the Saturday vigil Mass, Diane and I discussed the details of preparing for Christmas. With a three-month-old and a three-year-old, the details were exhausting.

We had to make sure we had diapers, formula, shampoo, and wipes. We purchased two car seats, a high chair, and bedding that still needed setup. As Mass began, I couldn't help but think about everything that I still needed to do.

That's when my friend Deacon Roger's homily hit home!

Deacon Roger was teaching a religion class at the grade school next door to the church. He explained that the four weeks preceding Christmas was a liturgical season.

He asked the second graders, "Do you know the name for this season?" ...Silence.

"All right then, how about a clue? The season starts with the letter A." Again, silence.

Once again he added, "The second letter is D."

This time Andrew, from the back of the classroom, threw up his hand! "I know," he exclaimed. "Advil!"

After the congregation stopped laughing, I asked myself if my season had been Advent or Advil. That day, it was Advil!

How do we keep the season more Advent and less Advil? Here are a few things we can try:

Let's block out some time each day to be quiet and enjoy the day. I like to sit in our living room and reflect on the manger scene on the coffee table.

In the anticipation of out-of-town guests, we get fixated on everything that we need to do. Let's not get hung up on the details and miss enjoying their presence. The details will all work out.

I am going to work hard at keeping the season about Advent. How about you? Are you in the middle of the Advent season or the Advil one?

Thanks, Deacon Roger, for the reminder!

Reflections: Has your Advent season become an Advil season? What can you do to make Advent a blessed season? Do you block out some time for reflection during Advent?

Behold!

*"The next day he saw Jesus coming toward him and said,
"**Behold**, the Lamb of God, who takes away the sin of the
world." –John 1:29*

*"The angel said to them, "Do not be afraid; for behold, I
proclaim to you good news of great joy that will be for all the
people." — Luke 2:10*

*"And behold, I am with you always, until the end of the
age." –Matthew 28:20*

One of my favorite words from the bible is
behold. In some older translations it is use almost
1300 times. Many of the newer translations use the
word less. The meaning is never more relevant
than in this distracted world we live in today.

Everyone is distracted. Soccer practice, school
plays and gymnastics; it is a wonder we can behold
anything.

Many people are disgusted with social media. They
are contemplating taking a break from Facebook,
Instagram Twitter and others platforms. Advent is
the perfect time to do this. The average person
spends close to 3 hours a day with social media. "I
just don't have the time" seems like a poor excuse.

Advent is just a month away and a great time for each of us to spend some time to reflect on our relationship with our Lord. We need to find some time to behold!

To behold means to give something our undivided attention. Take our relationship with God.

Luke asks us to ponder the angel's statement to Mary to **behold** the good news.

In John's gospel, John the Baptist asks us **to behold** the Lamb of God, Who takes away the sins of the world.

And, Jesus' statement in Matthew to **behold** the fact that He will be with us always until the end of time.

Many people think that Lent is the time of year for reflection. Advent gives us a time to prepare ourselves for the coming of our Lord on Christmas day. Let's promise ourselves that we will spend some time pondering the Word of God. Let's reflect on our relationship with the Lord. And, take a needed break from social media and the distractions in our daily lives.

So, how do we do it? How do we make some time for God?

1. We need to cut back on social media! Try going on Facebook only twice a day. And, shut of the notifications from Facebook

and other social media platforms. If you are like most people you can gain an hour throughout the day to just behold!

2. Use you time in the car driving to and home from work as a time of prayer and reflection. It will make you workday less stressful and will return you home in a good mood.

3. Read at least one good inspirational book during advent. There are many wonderful Catholic and Christian authors. A visit to your favorite books store should help you find something that suits your needs.

4. Spend some quiet time in prayer and reflection each day. Try to make a weekly Holy Hour, or attend a weekday Mass besides Mass on Sunday.

So, how about it? Let's promise each other that we will avoid all the noise and distractions. Let's spend some time this Advent season with our Lord. I promise it will make your Christmas holiday better than ever. We will **Behold** "*the good news of great joy that will be for all the people. For today in the city of David a savior has been born for you who is Messiah and Lord.*"

Have a blessed Advent.

Scripture: "*The next day he saw Jesus coming toward him and said, "**Behold**, the Lamb of God, who takes away the sin of the*

Reflections: Look up the word behold in the dictionary. Spend ten minutes today pondering its meaning.

The Power of Yes

Mary said, "Behold, I am the handmaid of the Lord. May it be done to me according to your word." Then the angel departed from her. — Luke 1:38 (NAB)

Such was his intention when, behold, the angel of the Lord appeared to him in a dream and said, "Joseph, son of David, do not be afraid to take Mary your wife into your home. For it is through the Holy Spirit that this child has been conceived in her. — Matthew 1:20 (NAB)

"Yes" is a word with tremendous power. It can unlock amazing opportunities, open doors, and lead us to a richer, fuller and more vibrant life.

In a marriage proposal, it can be the beginning of a lifetime of happiness.

In a job offer, it can be the beginning of a new career.

Saying "yes" to an idea can launch a new discovery, invention or cure.

In the gospel of Luke, a young virgin is asked by the angel Gabriel to bear God's son. Mary was troubled at what the angel said, and she pondered his words carefully. She was confused because she was a virgin.

But, in Mary's troubled confusion, fearful as she pondered what was being said, her response was "may it be done to me according to your word."

Mary said "Yes." Salvation history began with that yes!

> Let us look at her, and let us look to her, in order to be more humble, and even more courageous in following the Word of God, to receive

the tender embrace
of her son Jesus, an
embrace that gives
us life, hope, and
peace. — Pope
Francis [14]

Her betrothed, Joseph was a righteous man. In the gospel of Matthew, not wanting to expose Mary to shame, he decided to divorce her quietly. But when an angel appeared to him in a dream and asked that he take Mary as his wife, his response was "yes!" And, he named him Jesus, just as the angel instructed.

Yes is a powerful word, indeed. It can change the course of history.

Both Mary and Joseph were scared, confused, and felt unworthy. They struggled and pondered what was said and were free to say "no." They trusted God and gave themselves over to God's plan for their lives.

During Advent, God invites us to follow him. However, the decision is ours because of our free will. We are free to choose.

We are scared, feel unworthy, and struggle with what it means to truly follow Jesus. We ponder how our lives will be changed if we trust God and give ourselves over to His plan for our lives.

Do we have the faith to respond to God's call with a "Yes?" Are we willing to take a leap of faith that might lead us to a richer, fuller, more vibrant way of life?

With our "Yes" we can nurture the word of God within us. Like Mary and Joseph, we are called to bring forth a Savior to a weary, troubled world.

We live in a weary world. People are scared, confused, struggling and pondering their own life's decisions. The world is waiting for our "Yes."

Your "yes" can help change the course of history.

Mary and Joseph's "Yes" proposes to each of us a new way to live; a way of surrender to the Word made Flesh who dwells among us here and now.

This Advent, let us echo Mary and Joseph's "yes!" Your single "Yes!" might just change the world.

Reflections: *Have you said yes to Jesus? How did Mary and Joseph's yes make you examine your own commitment? How do you say yes, every day to Our Lord?*

Not a Bead, But a "Glory Be!"

> 'For I know the
> plans I have for
> you,' declares the
> Lord, 'plans to
> prosper you and
> not to harm you,
> plans to give you
> hope and a future.'
> – Jer. 29:11 (NAB)

Several times a year, our parish does a living rosary. Each person represents a bead on the rosary, and they form a human chain around the entire church representing each decade. One by one, they approach the statue of the blessed mother and recite their Our Father or Hail Mary.

I have attended several of these beautiful living rosaries over the years, but I never recall being asked to be a bead. I think I was an assistant bead once. That is a person who accompanies the bead but doesn't get to say anything. That's tough for me!

While I was humorously bemoaning the fact that I have been overlooked as bead material over the years, my friend, Deacon Roger overheard my whining.

He told me the story of a young boy who was also overlooked when the sisters at the school selected the kids to be beads at the school living rosary.

"Sister", he moaned. "I have never been a bead."

The wise and compassionate nun said, but you are a "Glory Be!"

A "Glory Be," the young man asked with a confused look on his face.

"Yes," sister replied. "Glory Be" is said on the chain between the beads, and we both know that the chain holds the entire rosary together! So, you have a very important role."

"That's it," I thought. Just like the little boy, I am a 'Glory be', and I can help hold the rosary together.

Now if I can only get over being picked last as a first grader playing "The Farmer in the Dell!" I guess I prefer being a 'glory be' to "the cheese!"

Reflections: *Is there any background activity you are involved with, rather than being in the spotlight? Do you ever feel more gratitude when you are not in the limelight?*

An Irregular Guy

Father, God chose the foolish of the world to shame the wise, and God chose the weak of the world to shame the strong, and God chose the lowly and despised of the world, those who count for nothing, to reduce to nothing those who are something, so that no human being might boast before God. It is due to him that you are in Christ Jesus, who became for us wisdom from God, as well as righteousness, sanctification, and redemption, so that, as it is written, "Whoever boasts, should boast in the Lord." —
1Corinthians 1:27-31 (NAB)

The seasons are changing, and for the first time this season, it was cold enough to wear a coat. As I scanned the coats in the hall closet, I spotted a nice-looking black coat that I never noticed before. I removed it from the hanger and saw that it still had the sales tags on it. It was new! My wife bought me a new coat, and I didn't even know it.

As I slipped the coat on, I noticed that it fit perfectly. But, to my dismay, as I went to zip it up, I noticed that the zipper was backwards. It had been sewn in wrong. As I looked at the tag, my suspicions were correct. This wonderful coat was an irregular!

Irregular, a word from my youth, still stings when I hear it. I grew up in a blue-collar family. My mom did most of my clothes shopping in the bargain basement of the local men's store. She shopped in the "irregulars department."

As a naive kid, I never knew what an irregular meant. I thought it was a brand name! I can still remember the embarrassment. The kids at school were comparing their brand name clothes. "My shirt is an Izod," said one kid. "Mine is a Calvin Klein," said another. The discussion went on until it was my turn.

"My shirt is an Irregular!" I proudly announced to a huge outburst of laughter. The laughter subsided as we made our way to class.

That night, I shared the story with my mom.

"What is an irregular?" I asked.

"Well, honey," she said as she paused to measure her words. "An irregular is a shirt, or pair of pants, with a slight flaw. Nothing big, or noticeable, but the prices are more affordable."

"You know son, the men Jesus picked for his apostles were all flawed. Each of the apostles were flawed in some way. And most of the saints didn't start out as saints. They were flawed, too, and they were able to overcome their flaws with God's grace."

She was doing her best to explain, but it wasn't working for me. I was still embarrassed to be the only kid in my class that was an irregular.

Now, as an adult, I can see the beauty in her wisdom. I realize that I am flawed. We are all flawed. For one thing, I am a sinner. And, only through God's grace and forgiveness, can I ever get to heaven.

I'm flawed in many other ways as well. I am balding and losing my hearing. I wear bifocal contacts, have bad knees, and a huge scar on my stomach from colon surgery. Come to think of it, I am a pretty irregular guy!

It is often said that God doesn't choose the qualified, he qualifies the chosen. I don't need to be perfect to serve Him. Just look at those apostles my mom mentioned. They were fishermen, tax collectors, men of no distinction. Yet, they went out and evangelized the entire world.

As I struggled to zip up my crazy zipper, I realized that being an irregular guy wasn't that bad. I'm going to wear my new jacket with humility and pride.

I know I'm flawed, but I'm happy to be an Irregular Guy!

Reflections: *Are you an irregular, too? Does salvation come from understanding that we are all flawed, and thus in need of being saved?*

Are You the One?

> When John heard in prison of the works of the Messiah, he sent his disciples to him with this question, "Are you the one who is to come, or should we look for another?"
> — Matthew 11:2-3 (NAB)

Doubts, We all have them at times. As Christians, we are embarrassed by our doubt. Is the story of Jesus true? Did he really die for my sins?

Noah had doubts when he built the Ark.

Abraham had doubts when he offered to sacrifice his son Isaac.

Moses had doubts when he led his people across the Red Sea.

David had doubts when he faced Goliath.

We know Blessed Mother Teresa had doubts, as she wrote about her "dark night of the soul."

Even John the Baptist, arguably the greatest prophet of the bible asked the Lord, "are you the one who is to come?"

Jesus, in Matthew's gospel, said that "among those born of women there has been none greater than John the Baptist." (Matthew 11:11) Yet, as John rotted away in prison, even he had doubts.

As we prepare for the coming of Jesus during Advent, we can use this time to read, study, talk to friends who have a strong faith, confess our sins and recommit ourselves to living a Christ-like life.

> "Everything is possible to one who has faith." Then the boy's father cried out, "I do believe, help my unbelief!"
> — Mark 9:23-24 (NAB)

What most people fail to realize is that doubt is not the opposite of faith. Disbelief is the opposite of faith. Doubt can actually build our faith and be the catalyst for spiritual growth, because it causes us to question things, and as a result learn truth.

Doubt is not sinful and unforgivable. God is big enough to handle all our questions. Doubt does not indicate a lack of faith, but a desire to have our faith grow.

Here are a few things to remember:

God is kind and merciful. He is patient with us and wants us more than we know. Like the father of the prodigal son, all we need to do is move in his direction and He will rush to greet us!

> So, he got up and went back to his father. While he was still a long way off, his father caught sight of him, and was filled with compassion. He ran to his son, embraced him and kissed him. — Luke 15:20 (NAB)

Our struggles bring new growth in faith. If we are doubt- free, we must already be in heaven! As for us earthlings, if we move in the direction of light, and not darkness, then, even in our doubt, we move closer to God.

In prayer, it's OK to admit our doubt and tell God how we feel. We can ask God to "help my disbelief." God will never give up on us. In His compassion and patience, He will wait for us and bless our searching.

Advent is a time to discover a closer and more intimate relationship with our Lord; to confront our doubts and turn them into a stronger, more vibrant faith. By doing so, we can then answer John the Baptist's question, "Are you the one?" with a resounding "Yes!"

On Christmas morning, Jesus, the One, has come into the world, our Savior, born of a virgin in Bethlehem.

Halleluiah!

Reflections: *Do you think your doubt is a lack of faith? What do you think of Tony's idea that doubt can lead to a greater faith? What will you be doing during Advent to grow your faith?*

The Winter Coat

Give and gifts will be given to you, a good measure, packed together shaken down and overflowing, will be poured into your lap. Luke 6:38

Growing up in a blue collar family, having a new coat for winter was a welcomed gift. That is one of the reasons I fondly remember my Aunt Jay. Each year, she would scrimp and save from her 90-cent an hour job at the dry cleaners. She would use the money to buy winter coats for my cousins, Diane, Steven, and Susan, and my sister Angie and me. And, believe me; it takes a lot of hot sweaty hours in the laundry to pay for five coats. But she did, and it wasn't until I became an adult that I realized just what a sacrifice that was.

My wife, Diane works with the Embrace Clinic and Care Center. Diane was in charge of their Christmas room a few years ago. The center provided coats and winter clothing for the children of their clients. They provided toys and gifts as well.

One day I read in the paper that a local Penny's outlet was selling coats at a low price. Remembering Aunt Jay, this was my opportunity to pay it forward and provide coats for needy kids. One Saturday morning, Diane and I made our way to the outlet. Just as advertised, there were nice winter coats in all sizes. I was like a kid in a candy store loading up two shopping carts with coats in a variety of sizes and colors.

The store was crowded with shoppers that day and the checkout lines were long. As I maneuvered the carts through the store, a young clerk was opening another checkout. She motioned me toward her checkout. I rushed to make my way and was the first in line at the new checkout. As I did I noticed that the young checkout girl was pregnant and her eyes were red from crying.

I smiled and tried to make some small talk when she asked me, "Wow, you have a lot of coats here, where are you taking them?"

"To the Embrace Clinic and Care Center," I replied. "What is that, she inquired?"

As I explained, her tears returned as she began to tell her story. "I'm pregnant and my parents kicked me out of the house. My boyfriend left and all I have is this part-time job and a room I am renting. I don't know how I will ever support a child, I need everything!

Immediately, Diane jumped in to the conversation, telling her that there was help. She gave her a card with the address and number of the center and told her to call on Monday and make an appointment.

Not long after that day, she had her baby, a big healthy boy. And she got the help she needed from this wonderful organization. She received a crib, layette, blankets, formula, and diapers. And, she received the spiritual help from a caring staff and volunteers were all waiting for her at the Embrace Clinic and Care Center.

I realized that our trip to the outlet that day to buy coats was a "God Appointment." We were meant to meet this beautiful young girl. And the fact that she opened the checkout line just for me, made it clear.

She got what she needed for her baby, and as a bonus, a coat for herself that was just the right size and color.

I could picture Aunt Jay, snapping her Juicy Fruit chewing gum, and smiling her special smile. She would pause and enjoy only for a moment, because then it would be time to start saving for next year.

CHAPTER THREE

....

Christmas

Christmas, the Happiest and Saddest of Times

The Christian faith can never be separated from the soil of sacred events, from the choice made by God, who wanted to speak to us, to become man, to die and rise again, in a particular place and at a particular time. — Pope Benedict XVI

Christmas day is fast approaching. For many people, it is the happiest and most joyful time of the year. The family assembles for a fantastic meal. The Christmas tree is surrounded by gifts. And, the relief that the shopping and gift wrapping is finally over and everyone can relax. It's time to enjoy the day.

For others, Christmas can be the saddest time of the year. Their minds turn to a loved one that they lost this year, a parent, grandparent, spouse or close friend. This is especially true if they lose a loved one during the holidays. That feeling can be relived for many years that follow.

There are those people who lose their job at years end as companies downsize to meet the challenges and uncertainty of a new year. Others have been unemployed and the job search hasn't turned up any leads. Those people are more concerned about making the mortgage payment and feeding their family than they are of gifts they don't need and can't afford.

Others suffer from social isolation and are alone for the holidays. The elderly in nursing homes, men and women serving in the military thousands of miles from home, and those who have started new careers far from family and can't make it home for the holidays.

Still others, it is a separation or divorce that changes the dynamic of the season for everyone affected by it.

Whatever the circumstances, the thought of a Merry Christmas is the farthest thing from their mind.

What can you do if you are saddened by any of these things?

Here are a few suggestions;

1. If you are alone or lonely, find out if your church or community center is having a get-together and make it a point to attend.

2. Volunteer at a homeless shelter or soup kitchen serving others and try to engage them in conversation.

3. Call some old friends on the phone, simply to wish them a Merry Christmas. You might find they are lonely too, and you'll be a blessing to them.

4. Try to think of the positive thing that God has blessed you with this past year. Often, counting our blessings can take our minds off the things that are making us sad.

5. Attend mass on Christmas, focusing your thought on the real meaning of Christmas. It will help in more ways than I can describe.

And what can the rest of us do to help?

1. Be kind. Understand that not everyone finds the holidays as joyous and happy as you might think they should.

2. Think of someone in your family or community that will be alone. It can be a widow or widower, a single or recently divorced parent, or someone that has lost a loved one recently. Invite them to your home for dinner and boost their spirits with a few laughs and conversation. Or shed a few tears as you ask them to share with you their memory of their lost loved one.

3.   If there are activities at your church or in your community that you will be attending, invite them to come along. A Christmas concert, luncheon or gift exchange might help make their day happier.

I am not alone at all, I thought. I was never alone at all. And that, of course, is the message of Christmas. We are never alone. Not when the night is darkest, the wind coldest, the world seemingly most indifferent. *For this is still the time God chooses. —Taylor Caldwell*

As you enjoy Christmas with your family and friends, let us not forget those who are lonely, sad, bereaved, without jobs, family, and friends or even hope.

During Advent, I pray daily for those people who find Christmas a difficult time of the year. I pray that hearts will be healed, that jobs will be found, that men and women in the military will return safely to their loved ones. I pray for the alone and lonely, in nursing homes and elsewhere. I pray for those with life threatening illnesses, who are worried that this might be their last Christmas. And, I pray for those with mental illnesses and depression that the Lord blesses them in a special way this Christmas.

And, I pray for you, my friends! May God bless you and heap his abundant blessing upon you and grant you His precious gift of peace.

Your Presence is Your Present

And the Word became flesh and made his dwelling among us, and we saw his glory, the glory as of the Father's only Son, full of grace and truth. John 1:14

At our Christmas Mass at the jail Tuesday night, the celebrant Father Lee, a humble, on-fire dynamo from South Korea, said something in the homily that resonated with me. He said, "Your presence is your present."

As kids, presents are an important part of the Christmas season. Looking through toy catalogs, watching television for the newest must have toys, and dreaming of Santa Claus placing them under the tree, is at the center of the season.

But as we get older, the present isn't quite as important as the people we have around us. Family and friends become very important at Christmas time. There is not a parent alive that wouldn't trade even the biggest present for having their family together at the holidays. Sons and daughters, grand kids, and friends, are the best Christmas gifts. Their presence at your holiday is the best Christmas present you could receive.

And, our presence is the greatest gift we can give, as well. I mean being "really present" and attentive to what is happening to them in their lives, and not allowing our attention to drift to our job, health, or any other distraction. Being truly present!

It is said that there are three elements to giving; the giver, the recipient, and the gift itself. The least important is the gift. The interaction of the two people involved, their presence to each other is the real gift.

We have seen recently how a lifetime of gifts can disappear instantly, like the homes and belongings of the people affected by Hurricane Sandy, or worse yet, the loss of the "presence" of the 20 children and 6 teachers at Sandy Hook Elementary School in Connecticut. Their presence is only a memory now.

At Christmas, it is good to remember that God gave us a gift too, the gift of HIS presence in the gift of His Son, Jesus Christ. He became man, dwelt among us, sharing his presence with his family, his friends, the Apostles, and the people he touched during his ministry.

Jesus is still present today. Let us strive to be attentive to our Lord this Christmas as well, and make it a point to spend more time with Him, in praise, prayer, and adoration. Pray with me:

Lord, make me more attentive to the presence of the people around me this Christmas, my wife, children, and friends. Let me not be distracted by the hurried pace of the things of the secular world that are not important. Help me, Lord, to be more attentive to you as well, in my prayer life and in helping those less fortunate around me. Help me to spend this Christmas, attentive to the presence of the Holy Family, and my own family, this day. Their presence will be the best present I receive this Christmas.

God bless you, and have a blessed and merry Christmas and happy and healthy New Year!

Reflection: *Do you agree that receiving a present at Christmas isn't as important as the people around us? What can we do to shut out the secular pressure to buy more presents? Which is most important, the gift, the giver, or the recipient? How do you relate to Jesus as God's gift to use at Christmas? What can you do to keep Christ in Christmas.*

My Christmas Train

"Amen, I say to you, unless you turn and become like children, you will not enter the kingdom of heaven. Whoever humbles himself like this child is the greatest in the kingdom of heaven. And whoever receives one child such as this in my name receives me." Matthew 18:3-5

One of my oldest childhood Christmas memories (reinforced by an annual recall by my parents) was when I was six years old. All I wanted for Christmas was a Lionel Train set that I had been admiring in the 1954 Lionel catalog. On Christmas morning, there it was, along with other toys and the obligatory socks and underwear.

Before I opened the box my parents sat me down and told me that a neighbor boy's father had been laid off and his Mom and Dad couldn't afford presents for my friend. Wouldn't it be nice if I gave up one of my toys, so that he would have something under his Christmas tree?

Quite a load to drop on a six-year old! I thought it was a good idea and I figured I could go a while longer with the socks and underwear I owned.

"What should I do?" I asked. My Dad responded, "Think about what gift would make him the happiest and give him that one."

After a long pause, a few choked back tears, I decided that it was the train set that would make him happy and reluctantly I said, "It was the one thing I really wanted for Christmas, but it would be the gift that would make him happy, so he can have my train.

The proud look on my parents face is something I remember to this day.

As my Dad removed the train set box from under the tree, I began to open my gifts. As I torn the paper from the underwear, I noticed behind the tree a Lionel box, just like the one I had given up. It was the train set from the 1954 catalog that I wanted so badly!

My Dad had a good year at work, and was able to purchase two train sets, one for me and one for my friend. Giving up the toy was just a test to see if I would be willing to give mine up for someone in need. I realized that I had passed their unusual test and was relieved that I didn't offer up the socks instead.

Before you nominate me for sainthood, I have learned over the years that most six-year olds would pass this test. I constantly hear stories of proud parents telling of the compassion and selflessness of their young children.

So why only a few years later, the same children complain "It's not fair, EVERYONE has a cell phone? I want one too!" Or, "I'm the only kid I know that doesn't have an X-Box 360!"

It's the greedy, self-centered, modern world. We are barraged with Hollywood images of over indulgences. I wondered, is this new or has this been going on for a long time?

As I thought about it, I was reminded of the nativity story. In all of Bethlehem, not a single man or woman was willing to give up their bed for a pregnant woman who was about to give birth. Not one! It says something about how we see a need and ignore it. I'm comfortable too bad my Savior has to be born in a manger.

I wonder what would happen if you posed this question to a six-year old at Christmas, "If you knew that Mary had nowhere to go to have her baby, would you be willing to give them your bed for a night so Jesus could be born in comfort?

I bet they would all pass the test!

Over the years, I kept that train set, still in the original box. It has moved with me from apartment to apartment, and home to home, always reminding me that we must become like children and humble ourselves, if we truly believe in the message of the incarnation. What are you willing to give up?

Reflection: *Do you think that the six year old in your life would pass the test? How about your teenagers? Have you ever given up something that you wanted to help another in need? How did that make you feel?*

A Christmas Story: A $20 Dollar Shine

"If a man is called to be a street sweeper, he should sweep streets even as a Michelangelo painted, or Beethoven composed music or Shakespeare wrote poetry. He should sweep streets so well that all the hosts of heaven and earth will pause to say, 'Here lived a great street sweeper who did his job well.'" — Martin Luther King Jr.

After weeks of shopping, hanging ornaments, planning meals, and making arrangements for flights home, Christmas is finally here. The pressure, anxiety, and worry will soon be over. It's so easy to get so caught up in the hoopla and anticipation that we overlook the most important elements of the holiday.

As I was searching for something to write about this Christmas, something that might make this a better Christmas for you and me, I have to admit that I was so stressed that nothing came to mind. These were the thoughts that went through my mind as I made the first of three trips to the airport on Christmas Eve.

I arrived about 15 minutes before my son Matthew's flight was to arrive from Orlando. As I walked through the terminal, I passed an older gentleman in a stocking cap.

As our eyes met we exchanged Merry Christmas greetings and as we passed each other, he looked down and said in a confident voice, "I can put a Christmas shine on those shoes for you."

Surprised, I replied, "Maybe later, I've got to check on my son's flight."

As I sat down outside the restricted area waiting for his arrival, I looked up and there was a shoe shine stand a few yards away, and standing next to the stand was the gentleman with whom I had just exchanged Christmas greetings.

As he spotted me he smiled and asked, "Ready for that Christmas shine now?"

"Sure," I replied with a smile. "I've got about 15 minutes before my son's flight arrives.

As I climbed up to the seat on his stand, it felt great as I realized that this was the first time I had a chance to sit all day.

"How are you," I offered making small talk.

"Blessed, I'm very blessed," he replied.

With that he began to tell me that he was just released from the hospital a week ago and this was his first day back on the job. He had heart problems and wasn't expected to make it.

"It's a miracle that I am alive today and I am so grateful," he humbly said. "Now, it's Christmas Eve and I'm alive, my wife is home cooking, and my children and grandchildren will be at my house on Christmas day. This week could have been very sad, but God has blessed me with a second chance at life and this will be the best Christmas ever!"

As he applied the polish and brushed away at my shoes they began to take on a shine.

"Wow!" I exclaimed. "They look shinier than when I bought them."

"I'm just getting started," He replied. "Most shoe shine stands just brush and buff; I'll give them a spit shine."

As he continued to apply coats of polish and snap his cloth I asked, "How long have you been shining shoes?"

"53 years," he responded without missing a beat of the rhythm of the snapping cloth. "I started when I was 9 years old and I'm 62 now. I am proud of the job I do; I think I am the best in the business!"

After a few finishing touches he was done and I agreed that this was the best shoe shine I had ever seen. As I stepped down from the stand our eyes met again.

He questioned me, "Does that look like a $5 dollar shine to you?"

"No," I said. "It looks more like a $20 dollar shine to me," as I reached for my wallet and handed him a $20 dollar bill.

"Merry Christmas," He said humbly.

"A Blessed Christmas to you, your wife and family too!" I quietly responded as I noticed that my son's flight had just arrived.

Later that evening, as I stood near the manger in our living room, I began to reflect on our conversation.

I too, have had health scares and was here to enjoy the holiday.

I too, am grateful to be alive.

My wife was cooking, baking and preparing for Christmas Day.

I've been at a job I love for 58 years this coming January, and just like the shoe shine man, I feel that I am the best at what I do.

Standing before the manger scene, I realized that his humble gratitude had rubbed off on me, just as the dust and grime had been rubbed off my shoes. He had shined my heart at the same time he shined my shoes.

As my head bowed, a tear fell from my face onto my newly shined shoes and I could feel God's love shining in my heart.

And, that's my Christmas wish for you, my friend. May you be grateful to be alive, to be spending time with your family and proud of the work you do to support them, whether you are a doctor or a shoe shine man.

May the light of our Savior, Jesus Christ, the light of the world, shine in your heart, like the glow in my heart and the gleam of my $20 dollar shine.

Reflections:

Forgiveness, the Greatest Gift

"If you forgive others their transgressions, your heavenly Father will forgive you. But if you do not forgive others, neither will your Father forgive your transgressions." — *Matthew 6:14-15*

In just a few days we celebrate Christmas, and as we do we begin to experience the anticipation of the holiday. We look forward to being united with family and friends. We hustle to purchase and wrap the final presents. We prepare for the great meal we will share. We can't wait to continue the family traditions that have become an integral part of the season.

We recheck our shopping list and stress out over the possibility that we might have forgotten someone, someone that we love.

Could we be forgetting someone that we once loved, someone that hurt us, someone that we may have hurt? Is there someone that you haven't forgiven or asked to forgive you?

Yes, we try to put the incident or situation out of our mind, but somehow, at Christmas, it all comes back to us. And, it limits the joy and happiness that Jesus' birth should bring us. We are locked in a prison of unforgiveness.

In a spiritual sense, the greatest gift we have ever received from God, our Heavenly Father, is His Son, Jesus Christ. He became man, destined to suffer, die on the cross, and rise again for the forgiveness of our sins. Through Jesus, we are forgiven!

"In this is love: not that we have loved God, but that he loved us and sent his Son as expiation for our sins. Beloved, if God so loved us, we also must love one another." –John 1 4:9-10

That forgiveness comes with a price, we must forgive too! As Jesus' death on the cross unlocks the chains of our sinfulness, we are empowered by the Holy Spirit to forgive those who have hurt us.

So, who is it? Who is the one person in most need of your forgiveness? Whether you visit them, call them, e-mail them, or send a text message, forgive them! Isn't it time to put the past behind you? Isn't it time to look ahead, with our eye on the prize of heaven and everlasting life. Isn't it time for forgiveness?

Unlock the prison of unforgiveness that burdens your heart this time of year. Then, the celebration of Christ's birth will bring you joy and happiness greater than you ever imaged. It might just be the one gift you'll remember for a lifetime.

Merry Christmas!

Reflections: *Is there someone missing from your holiday because of a fight or misunderstanding years ago? Do you* *have a family member that has been hurtful that needs your forgiveness this Christmas? Do you see Tony's point about forgiveness being a gift?*

The Giving Tree

> Amen, I say to you, whatever you did for one of these least brothers of mine, you did for me. — Matthew 25:40 (NAB)

As we waited for Mass to begin, I noticed the Giving Tree had been set up in the chapel. For the uninitiated, the Giving Tree is a Christmas tree decorated with paper ornaments with the name, age, and sex of a needy person and something that they might like as a Christmas gift. Every year we take a few names and purchase gifts.

"Hey honey," I whispered. "We should get a few names from the Giving Tree while there are still lots to choose from."

"Not today," my wife Diane responded. "I want to wait until they have been picked over. I like to buy for the people that no one picks; you know, the leftovers. I really like doing something special for the people no one picks."

As I settled back into my seat, I realized what she said. We are very judgmental people. We even judge what disadvantaged person gets our help. I have been guilty of this myself. I guess it is alright to pick a child, or a person of a particular sex, or in reading the notes, someone that we feel good helping. But there are always a few that no one selects.

I was so proud of Diane! I learn from her non-judgmental attitude. As a matter of fact, she prefers the unwanted, the leftovers, those who no one felt worthy.

It reminded me that one of my heroes, Mother Teresa, quickly became a saint for just that reason. She picked those that no one wanted, to help.

She would say, "If you judge people, you have no time to love them." [4]

This Christmas season let's try to be less judgmental and help those who become the leftovers on the Giving Tree.

Reflections: *Have you ever been guilty of being judgmental when helping people? What do you think of*

Mother Teresa's observation that judging people gives us no time to love them? Do you participate in your Giving Tree?

But, Where's the Baby

"Now there were shepherds in that region living in the fields and keeping the night watch over their flock. The angel of the Lord appeared to them and the glory of the Lord shone around them, and they were struck with great fear. The angel said to them, "Do not be afraid; for behold, I proclaim to you good news of great joy that will be for all the people. For today in the city of David a savior has been born for you who is Messiah and Lord." –Luke 2:8-11

There is a story of two young women having an elaborate lunch together in an upscale downtown restaurant. As they are enjoying their food and conversation, the invited guest asks her friend the reason for the occasion.

She replies, "We are celebrating the baby's birthday!"

"But, where is the baby?" said her bewildered friend.

"Oh," said the mother, "You didn't think I would bring him, did you?" Why he doesn't know anything about it."

Isn't it the same for many people when it comes to the birth of Jesus? We all celebrate Christmas but many of us don't even invite Jesus to the party.

We obsess over every detail of the holiday; the tree, garland, Santa Claus, presents, colorful lights, a wonderful meal, and a great holiday party. Everything, that is, except Jesus, the reason for the season.

What is the point of celebrating Christmas, if we don't invite Jesus to the celebration?

"You can never truly enjoy Christmas until you can look up into the Father's face and tell him you have received his Christmas gift." –John R. Rice

What can we do as Catholics and as Christians to keep Christ in Christmas?

Here are a few ideas:

1. **Set up a nativity scene** in a prominent location in your home. And, keep it up during the 12 days of Christmas until the Epiphany. Have a tradition of placing baby Jesus in the manger on Christmas Eve. I am always impressed with the kids that visit us. They approach the manger with a reverence that only an innocent child can have as they look at the baby Jesus in the manger. Have Jesus visible and present.

2. **Attend Mass** on Christmas Eve or day. Make mass attendance at Christmas a family tradition. When we attended Christmas Eve mass we would return home and open just one gift that night. Somehow, I always selected the gift with the underwear and socks! It became a Christmas tradition.

3. **Light an Advent wreath** each week until Christmas day and spend a little time reading the Christmas story from Luke 1 1:5-56 and Luke 2:1-20 a portion each week. Make it brief but always centered around Jesus and the nativity story.

4. **Give God a special gift.** Christmas is a time to forgive someone that has hurt you. It's a great time to reach out to a family member or loved one that has been estranged from the family for whatever reason. Often, they are waiting and praying for a chance to reunite but someone has to take the initiative. It my experience, as time passes, we often can't even remember why they are estranged or the reason has become mute. Consider these acts of kindness a gift from you to God.

5. **Adopt a needy family** or take a few names from The Giving Tree. Or, send a Christmas card to someone serving our country in the military. Why not invite someone to Christmas dinner? Usually, there is plenty of food for another person or persons at the table. And, don't forget to say grace and give thanks.

I am sure that you can think of many other ways to keep Christ in Christmas and to start a few new Christmas traditions with your family, especially the kids.

If we are truly celebrating the birth of our savior then let's bring the baby to the party.

Reflections: What are the ways you are keeping Christ in Christmas?

Lord, make me more attentive to the people around me this Christmas, my wife children and friends. Let me not be distracted by the hurried pace if the things of the secular world that are not important. Help me, Lord, to be more attentive to you, as well, in my prayer life and in helping those less fortunate around me. Help me to spend this Christmas attentive to the presence of the Holy Family, and my own family, this day. Their presence will be the best present I receive this Christmas. --Tony Agnesi

No Nativity, No Eucharist

"And she gave birth to her firstborn son. She wrapped him in swaddling clothes and laid him in a manger, because there was no room for them in the inn." –Luke 2:7

Our living room is rarely used. It has become a place to go to make a quiet phone call, read or just get away from the noise and activity of the day. It's our quiet room.

It is also the place where my wife, Diane sets up the nativity scene each year, a place where I enjoy going to pray and reflect on the birth of our Savior.

As I contemplated the scene, I realized, for the first time, that the Eucharist was a continuation of the nativity, the continuation of Christmas.

The manger, a simple feeding trough, where the animals of the nativity scene were fed, held the same body of Jesus, the bread of life, that we feed on in the sacrament of the Eucharist.

The next morning, as I received communion at daily mass, for a moment, as I held the Blessed Sacrament in my cupped hand, I realized that I held Jesus, body and blood, soul and divinity, the same Jesus born in a manger that first Christmas day. My hands represented the manger and for a moment, as I held Jesus in my hand, my mind returned to the manger scene where I had prayed the night before.

In that moment, the stable where Jesus was born became the tabernacle and the manger became the ciborium. And, it became clear that we owe the Blessed Sacrament to Bethlehem. No nativity, no Eucharist!

Jesus said to them, "I am the bread of life; whoever comes to me will never hunger, and whoever believes in me will never thirst. —John 6:35

Bethlehem, the city of Christ's birth, Beit Lehem (לחם בית) is Hebrew for "House of Bread." How appropriate that our Savior, Jesus Christ, the Bread of Life, would be born in a city known as the "house of bread."

We realize that the bodily presence of Jesus, made incarnate that Christmas morning in Bethlehem, is the same presence, body, blood, soul and divinity that we share in the Eucharist.

Every time we receive the Eucharist, we are given the opportunity to "lay him in a manger."

Over the years, volumes have been written about keeping Christ in Christmas, about continuing the Christmas spirit not just on December 25th, but every day of the year. We pray that we can somehow make every day Christmas day.

Help us Lord, to realize that we can do just that. We can do it in the reception of the Eucharist! The Jesus, the Bread of Life, we receive, is the same body, blood, soul and divinity, born that first

Christmas morning in the tabernacle of a stable and the ciborium of the manger.

Join with me, my friend, as we celebrate Christmas, not just on Christmas day, but all year long in the frequent reception of the Eucharist.

We make physical resolutions: lose weight, exercise more, so that we might live longer.

We make spiritual resolutions, prayer, forgiveness, humility, kindness, so that we might live forever. --Tony Agnesi

CHAPTER FOUR

The New Year

More or Less

Do not conform yourselves to this age but be transformed by the renewal of your mind, that you may discern what is the will of God, what is good and pleasing and perfect. — Romans 12:2 (NAB)

I'm not a fan of New Year's resolutions, but I do like to take some time at the end of the year to set goals. Resolutions are great, but we rarely follow through on them and that can make us feel like failures.

Why not try something different this year? Decide what you want to do less, then, find something opposite and positive that you want to do more.

Then, take some baby steps in the new direction. Here are a few examples of what I am going to try to do less of this year and what I want to do more.

I want to **complain less and express appreciation more**. There is something addictive about complaining. There is always something to complain about and for many people complaining is what they do all day. What we need to do is focus our attention on appreciation. You might find that there are just as many things to be grateful for as there are things to complain about.

I want to gossip less and praise more. You can always find a group of people who will spend their time gossiping about anyone who isn't there. They suck you in to their conversations, kill your positive attitude and compel you to join in. Learn to counter their gossip with praise. Praise someone who did something nice for you; someone who helped you with a project at work or offered a helping hand when you were in need.

I want to procrastinate less and take action more. It's amazing how fast time passes. That project you were going to do last January never happened. And, now it's a year later and you still haven't begun. Create fewer objectives and get to work on them now. You'll find that you'll get more done by attempting less.

I want to say less and listen more. Often, we have a lot to say and we want to share our knowledge to add to the conversation. We also need to know when to be quiet and listen. People want to share their story, telling you what's going on in their lives. Give them some time to share. You'll find that they will be more interested in what you have to say if you listen first.

I want to eat less and exercise more. This coming year I want to carve out time to exercise and do it. I never miss a meal (hardly ever), so why should I miss an opportunity to get some physical activity? I want to tip the scales to less eating and more activity. As a result, the scale should show a smaller number this time next year.

I want to get angry less and show kindness more. Anger is a banquet and you are the entrée. Anger eats away at you, destroys your health and well-being, and causes stress. Kindness is relaxing. It improves your health and well-being, and calms stress.

I want to judge less and accept more. We love to judge people. We are annoyed by their flaws and misgivings. We need to learn to accept them, flaws and all, just as God accepts us, just as we are, with all our flaws.

> Only if you
> thoroughly reform
> your ways and your
> deeds; if each of you
> deals justly with his
> neighbor; if you no
> longer oppress the
> resident alien, the
> orphan, and the
> widow; if you no
> longer shed
> innocent blood in
> this place, or follow
> strange gods to your
> own harm, will I
> remain with you in
> this place, in the
> land which I gave
> your fathers long
> ago and forever. —
> Jeremiah 7:5-7
> (NAB)

There are so many other things that I could add.

Watch television less and read more.

Frown less and smile more.

Fear less and love more. I am sure that you can think of many others to add.

This holiday season let's make sure to take some time to set goals. Use that time to think about what you want to change in your life next year. Meditate on what you want to do less and what you want to do more. Write them down and then get to work on making it happen. It will be a gradual change, as less of a negative thing is replaced with a more positive one.

Come on, you can do it! We'll do it together.

Reflections: What do you want to do more and less? What are a few of your goals for positive change? What changes do you want to make this year?

The List

Every late December, I sit down and plan my goals for the coming year. It is my way of handling the New Year's resolution issue. I've been doing it for most of my adult life.

I found over the years that New Year's resolutions lasted only a few days or weeks at best, but GOALS were always there in from of me. I would write down each goal, a list of around ten in all, on a small piece of paper that I would carry with me in my wallet.

As I traveled with my job, bored in a hotel room, I would often open my wallet to look at the pictures of my wife and young children, and there it would be, the list!

As I opened the paper and began to read, I was amazed that I had actually accomplished a few of the goals on my list! But, there were always a few things that still eluded me. I would be a bit embarrassed, because the list meant accountability, but I was also reenergized to work on the remaining ones.

I divided the list into three sections. First, my health goals! Lose weight, control my blood pressure, work-out more frequently, thing like that.

Then, I would look at personal goals, being a better husband, father, friend, and what specific things I was going to do to accomplish these. It's not as simple as, I'm going to be a better father. It means, I am going to do these specific things on this time table to be a better father.

Then professional goals. Things I wanted to accomplish. Start a new business, become a blogger, change jobs, get a promotion, and many others.

And finally, my spiritual goals like attend mass more often, read the bible daily, pray the Liturgy of the Hours, recite a rosary or chaplet every day, and then hold myself accountable to these goals.

If it made it to the list, then, the goal was in stone!

This past month, I realized that the year was half over. It prompted me to open up my wallet and take out the list. As I read down the items, I was really pleased at what I had accomplished, but challenged by the few I hadn't done or even begun. A small reminder of what I had promised myself, my family, my work and my God.

Now it's back to work! I've still got six months to complete the list. And with God's help, I will.

Living Your Resume or Eulogy?

I conducted a time management seminar for around 40 people. Whenever I make this presentation, I ask the group "Why do you want to manage your time better?" The responses are varied but most revolve around time famine. They want to get more done, make more money or get a better job.

How about managing our time so that we might devote it to things that are really important?

"Are You Living Your Eulogy or Your Résumé?" I'll ask.

Usually, there are few confused faces, because it is a question that many have never been asked.

A recent Huffington Post article talked about redefining success, beyond power and money to include well-being, wisdom and our ability to wonder and to give, as part of the equation. They call it the Third Metric.

When we remember someone who died, we rarely talk about their money and power achievements. We talk about the quality of their character, what they believed, how they treated others or their strong faith.

We don't recall their number of Facebook friends, the number of times they reviewed the sales figures, or that they never missing a reality show. We remember things like Joe was a good husband, father, and friend. Or, Mary cared about the poor, less fortunate, the sick and the aged.

In managing our time, we must differentiate between things that are important and things that are urgent. Things like e-mail, texting, smart phones, Facebook and Twitter are all made to seem important because their immediacy creates a false sense of urgency.

Their urgency doesn't make them important! As a matter of fact they are the greatest time wasters!

Last week, I saw a man in a swimming pool with his kids, but he was wearing his blue tooth headset in the water, just in case someone called. Is it that he considers the smart phone more important that some quality time with his kids or has he simply become so narcissistic that being connected with work is more important than being connected with his children? Teens will text their friends hundreds of times a day, instead of getting on their bicycle and spending some time together.

What would happen if we talked to a fellow worker face to face instead of texting them? What would happen if we took half the time we spend on Facebook and visited someone in the hospital, Grandma at the nursing home or served food and a local shelter?

We would be living our Eulogy instead of our resume! We would be defining our success by the Third Metric of well-being, wisdom and our ability to wonder and to give back.

Catholic author Matthew Kelly often speaks of the goal of becoming "the best version of yourself" that you can. Isn't that what our Lord is asking of us? To do that, we must realize that the best version of ourselves isn't how quickly we can respond to a text message, or how many e-mail's we get each day, or by the number of our Facebook friends. It is how we use our gifts for the glory of God.

Take the Eulogy test. How would you like your life to be described at your funeral? It is not too late to change gears and make your life matter!

Business philosopher and author Jim Rohn said, "We all have two choices: We can make a living or we can design a life." We can discover this by asking the question, "What gives meaning to my life?"

That answer will reveal the best, most authentic version of you. Live that and you'll be living your eulogy instead of your resume.

Reflection: *If you were to die today, how would you like your life to be described at your funeral?*

Beginning Today

Remember not the events of the past, the things of long ago consider not; See, I am doing something new! — (Isaiah 43:18—19, NAB)

Have you ever said to yourself, I wish I knew back then what I know now! I would do things differently. As we get older, we realize that we made many mistakes in the past, although we didn't know it then. We have regrets, but there is not much we can do about it. However, we can decide to live out our years differently.

One of my friends who is approaching eighty, made an important point. When we realize that the number of years we have left on earth are far fewer than those we have lived, we need to make these changes, beginning today!

What are the things I wish I knew when I was a younger man? Here are a few:

1. <u>Time flies!</u> As we get older time seems to go by quickly. I remember in high school that it would seem like an eternity for summer vacation to arrive. As an older adult, we wish the clock would slow down a bit. We realize that if we are going to make changes in our lives we have to do it now.

2. <u>Money doesn't equal success.</u> As a businessman, I have met many wealthy people with miserable lives. I have met people with very modest means who are happier and have real joy in their lives. We spend our adult lives accumulating money. We haven't enjoyed family, friends and memorable experiences. We may be too old or physically challenged to begin.

3. <u>Kids grow up quickly. We spend</u> our children's youth chasing money and success. We sacrifice the wonder and joy of watching our children grow. Those years, from babies and toddlers to adults we can never get back.

4. <u>Relationships are everything.</u> Making memories with our spouse is one of the ways we keep our relationship fresh. Those memories will sustain us when we get older and lose our mobility. Our relationship with God is the most important relationships we have. Next to that our relationships with our spouse, children, extended family and friends. Take some time to nurture these

relationships. It can be as simple as a weekly call to your mother to say I love you.

Put away the old self of your former way of life, corrupted through deceitful desires, and be renewed in the spirit of your minds, and put on the new self, created in God's way in righteousness and holiness of truth. — (Ephesians 4:22— 24, NAB)

5. <u>Knowing about God is important, but not as important as knowing Him personally.</u> Churches overflow with older people who want a personal relationship with Our Lord.

6. <u>Prayer isn't for bad times.</u> An active prayer life is something we should be striving for, not only when we reach retirement. There is nothing wrong with praying in tough times. But, prayers of thanksgiving are also important when thing are going well.

7. <u>Align yourself with people who share your values.</u> Younger adults spend time trying to impress others. Many of those we try to impress have a different set of values than we do. Often, we compromise our own values to "fit in" with the in crowd. Relationships are much stronger with those who share our vales.

8. <u>Admit your mistakes.</u> We are all going to make mistakes. Younger adults spend too much time defending their mistakes. The effects linger for a long time. We have a saying in business, "fail fast." Admit your

mistakes and learn from them. It is part of the process of gaining maturity.

Knowing what we know now that we didn't know then, what changes can we make to do things differently? What can we do beginning today?

Beginning today—We can spend more time with our family. For starters, we can plan a weekly date night with our spouse. Giving up poker night to have a movie night with the kids, might be fun.

Beginning today—We are going to put relationships before the pursuit of money. A bigger house, more expensive car, or the Rolex watch, won't guarantee happiness.

Beginning today—We will spend more time with our children or grandchildren. We will collect memories that will last a lifetime.

Beginning today—We will pursuit a personal relationship with Jesus. All that we have is a gift from God and we express our gratitude in prayer.

Beginning today—We are going to admit our mistakes. We will make a vow to make the changes necessary to live a life of character and integrity.

How about you? Can you think of a few others? What are you going to do, beginning today?

A Giving Heart

"When he looked up he saw some wealthy people putting their offerings into the treasury and he noticed a poor widow putting in two small coins. He said, "I tell you truly, this poor widow put in more than all the rest; for those others have all made offerings from their surplus wealth, but she, from her poverty, has offered her whole livelihood." —Luke 21:1-4

There is a story of a young girl who was moved by the request of her preacher a few weeks before Christmas 50 years ago. The preacher mentioned from the pulpit that there was a family in their very small congregation that was down on their luck. The father was unemployed, the oldest child was ill, and every penny they had could hardly keep the family together.

"Wouldn't it be nice," he offered, "if the congregation would all bring in what they could next Sunday and present it to this wonderful family."

The young girl was determined to do whatever she could that week and would bring in any money she could accumulate to help them.

She tapped her piggy bank; she looked for loose change in the sofa cushions, and helped a neighbor with some chores to earn another dollar. All in all, she accumulated two dollars and 73 cents.

The next Sunday, as she walked down the center isle to drop off her $2.73 in the basket, she felt humble; embarrassed that she could only give this needy family less than 3 dollars.

At the end of the service, the preacher called the family up to the front to present the money that congregation had collected. To the young girls amazement it was her family!

I heard about this story from that same young girl, only now it was 50 years later and she was a successful business woman. She told the story from a banquet podium the night she was honored for her philanthropy, her generosity.

Her story reminded me of the poor widow's two small coins. She was generous even though she had very little to give.

To me, this story proves one thing; that generosity has nothing to do with a person's financial situation. A generous person is generous whether they are rich or poor.

In my experience, some of the most generous people I have ever met were people with very limited means. They give out of the kindness of their hearts, they give to be a blessing, they give out of a sense of gratitude, and they work so that they can have a chance to give. They realize that it is impossible to love without giving.

They truly have the heart of a giver. They realize that giving increases their happiness. They don't give in order to get. They have no selfish motives. And, they often give anonymously so as not to draw attention to themselves.

If I asked you who are the most Christ-like persons you know? Many would say my grandma, my mom, a special aunt, my father, or grandfather. The reason is they have a generous heart.

What can we do to have a giving heart? We can start by counting our blessings. Gratitude leads to generosity when we realize that no matter our circumstances, someone is suffering more.

This year, let's make it a goal to have a giving heart!

A Final Thought

We have come to the end of the stories, reflections and prayers. I hope that one or more have become a blessing to you. I pray that the book has, in some way, helped you to have a joyful holiday season.

May you share this beautiful season with family and friends as we anticipate the birth of Our Savior, Jesus Christ, and prepare our hearts for the coming year with gratitude and grace.

All net proceeds from the sale of this book, as well as the other books in this series, will go to the charities and ministries that my wife, Diane, and I support. I make no income from the sale of these books.

References

Chapter 1 – Thanksgiving

St Rose of Lima, virgin (Ad medicum Castillo: edit L. Getno, "The Patroness f America, Madrid 1928, pp. 54-55)

Samuel F. Pugh, (*A Thanksgiving Prayer* accessed November 4, 2023) https://www.appleseeds.org/thankgv5.htm

Stuber, Mary Arlis. "*Thank God for Dirty Dishes.*" Scrapbook.com https://www.scrapbook.com/poems/doc/723.html. (July 19, 2019)

Chapter 2 –Advent

Daniel Gabriel Rosetti (Quote) https://www.brainyquote.com/quotes/dante_gabriel_rossetti_304330#:~:text=Dante%20Gabriel%20Rossetti%20Quotes&text=The%20worst%20moment%20for%20the%20atheist%20is%20when%20he%20is,and%20has%20nobody%20to%20thank.

Francis, Pope (Angelus 8 December 2013 Accessed November 4, 2023)https://www.vatican.va/content/francesco/e

n/angelus/2013/documents/papa-
francesco_angelus_20131208.html

Chapter 3- Christmas

Benedict XVI, Pope Accessed November 4, 2023
https://www.brainyquote.com/quotes/pope_bene
dict_xvi_189019

Caldwell, Taylor Accessed November 4, 2023
https://www.goodreads.com/quotes/95399-i-am-
not-alone-at-all-i-thought-i-was

Agnesi, Tony (*Finding God's Grace*)
https://tonyagnesi.com/2018/12/lord-make-me-
attentive-2/

King, Martin Luther, *The King Center Organization,*
http://www.thekingcenter.org/blog/mlk-quote-
week-all-labor-u[lifts-humanity-has-dignity-and-
importance-and-should-be-undertaken, April 9,
2013

Agnesi, Tony (*Finding God's Grace*)
https://tonyagnesi.com/2018/12/resolutions/

Chapter 4- New Years

Huffington Post (Are you living your Resume or eulogy) Accessed November 4, 2023
https://www.huffpost.com/entry/are-you-living-your-eulogy-or-your-resume_b_3936937#:~:text=Even%20for%20those%20who%20die,current%2C%20broken%20definition%20of%20success.

Acknowledgements

There are so many people to thank for their help in both the writing and publishing of *A Storyteller's Guide to a Joyful Holiday Season.*

Since this book is curated from as far back as 2010 and includes materials from my award winning blog and podcast, stories taken from my three best-selling books and quotes and prayers taken from my Facebook feature Daily Grace many people need to be thanked!

Thank you to my wife Diane for her constant encouragement over the years, as well as her weekly spelling and grammar checks.

Thank you to Deacon Roger Klaas for his friendship and inspiration

Thank you to Chuck Eberhart for the photography, graphics, the cover art for the entire Storyteller series.

Thank you to my editors over the years, Molly Romano, Ginny Lieto, Michelle Buckman.

Thank you to Catholic Radio especially Living Bread Radio in Canton, Ohio, Annunciation Radio in Toledo, Ohio.

Other Books in The Storyteller's Series by Tony Agnesi

Web site: TonyAgnesi.com

A Storyteller's Guide to a Grace-Filled Life, Tony Agnesi, Wadsworth: Virtu Press, 2017.

A Storyteller's Guide to a Grace-Filled Life, Volume 2, Tony Agnesi, Wadsworth: Virtu Press 2019

A Storyteller's Guide to Joyful Service: Turning Your Misery into Ministry, Tony Agnesi, Wadsworth: Virtu Press, 2018.

Notes